Taking Steps

A Farce

Alan Ayckbourn

Samuel French—London
New York — Sydney — Toronto — Hollywood

Elizabeth (*closing and fastening the suitcase*) I think it's upstairs in the attic. Come and give me a hand, will you?

Elizabeth goes out of the master bedroom on to the landing, followed by Mark. During the next speeches, they climb the stairs to the attic bedroom

Mark Anyway, don't be too sure. Things have a way of turning out.

Elizabeth Oh, yes?

Mark *Vis-à-vis* me and Kitty, I mean.

Elizabeth Oh, good. (*Pausing on the stairs and shuddering*) Aarrgh! I shall be glad to leave this place. I hate it. Who else but Roland would ever dream of buying it.

Mark I thought you were the one who wanted to live here.

Elizabeth Me?

Mark Fancying yourself as lady of the manor, you know you did.

Elizabeth Rubbish. (*Trying the wall switch to the attic bedroom*) Damn, there's no light.

Mark Probably the bulb.

Elizabeth Is it?

Mark (*climbing on to a chair and inspecting the centre light socket*) Yes, yes, it's definitely the bulb.

Elizabeth How can you tell?

Mark There isn't one in here. (*Getting off the chair*) Surely this is the awful Mrs Porter's room?

Elizabeth The ex-Mrs Porter, yes. Knowing her, she probably took the bulb with her. Can you find the bed?

Mark Hang about. (*He gropes round*) I think so.

Elizabeth There should be a suitcase in that corner cupboard. Unless she's stolen that.

Mark Won't be a minute. (*He gropes about*) Is he definitely buying this place?

Elizabeth So he says. It's draughty, it leaks and it smells. It's a white elephant. Everyone says so. He's the laughing stock of the county.

Mark (*finding a suitcase*) Here we are. Got it.

Elizabeth Ugh, there's dust everywhere. She did nothing. He's well rid of her.

She starts back down the stairs to the master bedroom. Mark follows, carrying the empty suitcase

(*Stopping*) Oh, how I loathe this house. It has no music about it, has it?

Mark Hasn't it?

Elizabeth No, none.

Mark Seen the ghost yet, have you?

Elizabeth Don't be silly.

She returns to the bedroom. Mark comes in after her. Elizabeth takes the suitcase, puts it on the bed and starts to fill it with more belongings. Mark watches her, impatiently

Mark Look, how much longer are you going to be?

Elizabeth Just a minute.

Mark Because if I'm supposed to be running you to the station . . .

Elizabeth All right, all right.

Mark Well, will you get a move on.

Elizabeth I don't know why you're in such a hurry. What are you doing that's so important?

Mark I suppose I might as well tell you. (*He sits on the dressing-table stool*) I mean, I didn't mean to tell you. I didn't mean to tell anyone but the cat's half out of the bag already, so—the point is, Kitty is coming back.

Elizabeth Kitty?

Mark Yes.

Elizabeth Back here?

Mark Yes.

Elizabeth When?

Mark Today, actually. She's due to get off the train in about half an hour. I'm meeting her. Which is the reason why I can't hang around.

Elizabeth But why?

Mark Why what?

Elizabeth Why is she coming back here?

Mark It's her home for one thing. Her parents are here. I'm here.

Elizabeth But she'd just broken out. She'd found freedom.

Mark I don't call running off with a Cypriot waiter from *The Boar's Head* finding freedom.

Elizabeth I can't believe she'd want to come back here.

Mark Why not? I'm here.

Elizabeth Yes, I know that.

Mark Well. Automatic reaction.

Elizabeth Yes. Possibly. Still.

Mark Besides. I don't think she had any choice in the matter. She had to come back here. They bought her a ticket and put her on the train.

Elizabeth Who did?

Mark Three of them.

Elizabeth Who?

Mark Two policemen and a policewoman.

Elizabeth What happened?

Mark Oh, it's all—awful.

Elizabeth What did Kitty do?

Mark It's all—ghastly. Nothing. It's all—dreadful. Really foul. Terrible. Embarrassing. No. (*Pause*) She was—she was—there was some talk about a charge of soliciting.

Elizabeth Kitty?

Mark It was that little waiter from *The Boar's Head* who put her up to it, I'm sure of that.

Elizabeth Soliciting.

Mark Suspicion of. They arrested her in the middle of Haverstock Hill.

Elizabeth What an odd place to choose. I mean, up that end of London. Everybody there seems to have someone already.

Mark. Yes Well, that's the sorry story.

Elizabeth By the garage or further up?

Mark (*suddenly extremely angry and pacing about clenching his fists*) I honestly don't know, Lizzie, and I don't think it makes the slightest difference. The facts are, my fiancée was arrested on suspicion of soliciting. Isn't that enough? (*Looking at his watch*) Look, I have to go, her train's due. I can't wait. I'm sorry.

Elizabeth But I haven't even changed yet . . .

Mark Well, get yourself a taxi.

Elizabeth Out here? By the time I get one here, Roland'll be home from work and in bed. He's due back in an hour.

Mark Why didn't you get the whole thing organized a bit earlier, then? You've had all day to leave the man.

Elizabeth I didn't decide until lunchtime, did I?

Mark Well, I can't wait. Sorry.

Elizabeth But you're going to be here for Roland.

Mark How can I? I'll have Kitty with me . . .

Elizabeth You can drop her off at home. Then come back.

Mark I am not letting her out of my sight. I can't take her home with me to our place. Mother won't speak to her since our so-called wedding day. We can't go to her place because her parents won't speak to either of us.

Elizabeth Where are you both going?

Mark Well, actually I—booked us a couple of single rooms at *The Bull*.

Elizabeth *The Bull*? That pub off the ring road. That's an awful dump.

Mark I'm hardly going back to *The Boar's Head*. I don't fancy mixing with that waiter's relatives.

Elizabeth (*collecting the remaining bottles from the dressing-table*) Has she got some overnight things? If they picked her up in the middle of the road.

Mark No, I've got some for her. In a suitcase.

Elizabeth Where from?

Mark Well—it's her suitcase she packed for our honeymoon actually. After she took off and bolted, it somehow got left in the boot of my car. Never been unpacked since. Hadn't got the heart to.

Elizabeth How sad.

Mark Yes. (*He sits on the stool*)

Elizabeth (*sitting on the bed*) It'll all be dreadfully creased. (*During the following speech Elizabeth dozes off*)

Mark (*suddenly deflated and rather depressed*) What it all adds up to, Lizzie, the thing is with you and really in a way I suppose it's the same with me, it's in the blood. When we were kids, I always had this dilemma over personal relationships. I always drew back from them, fighting shy of getting too deeply involved with someone, possibly fear of getting hurt, I don't know. I think that's probably true in my case. When I first met Kitty, things were very much that way. Certainly to start with. Still are, I suppose. Funny. I never really talk like this to anyone. (*He pauses*)

She awakes with a snort

Elizabeth What?

Mark Eh?

Elizabeth God, I dozed off.

Mark Oh, did you?

Elizabeth Sitting here, I actually nodded off to sleep. (*She rises*) You can see the sort of state I'm in. I must be totally exhausted. Sorry, were you saying something?

Mark No. Look at the time, I must dash. (*He moves to the bedroom door, then turns, puzzled*) That's always happening to me these days, you know. I'm chatting away and people just seem to doze off. Happening more and more lately. Is it something to do with my tone of voice, do you think?

Elizabeth I shouldn't think so.

The front doorbell rings downstairs

Who on earth's that?

Mark No idea at all.

Elizabeth Have a look. Get rid of them.

Mark O.K.

Elizabeth Don't tell them I'm here, anyway.

Mark Righto.

Mark goes down the main staircase, across the hall, and to the front door. Elizabeth gets on with her packing. Mark opens the front door

Tristram enters. He is about twenty-five, young, eager and pleasant. He wears a dark, sober raincoat and a discreet suit. He carries a briefcase.

After a few moments Elizabeth goes out to the bathroom

Mark Yes?

Tristram Yes.

Mark Yes?

Tristram (*very flustered*) Yes. (*He steps further into the hall*)

Mark closes the front door

Sorry. My name's . . . No. I'm from Speake, Tacket and—er—Whatsname . . .

Mark What?

Tristram Sorry. Hot. I'm—my name's—er—well, I'm here on behalf—on behalf of Mr Winthrop who's been—er—taken ill, you see. Not seriously. So, I'm here instead.

Mark Who's Mr Winthrop?

Tristram Oh, he's—Mr Crabbe'll know him. He's from . . . You're not Mr Crabbe?

Mark No, I'm Mr Boxer.

Tristram Right. Sorry. Mr Boxer. Well, he—that is, Mr Winthrop—he's from Speake and Winthrop. No. Rather—sorry—Speake, Tacket and Winthrop. Where I am also am from.

Mark (*distinctly puzzled*) You're expected, are you?

Tristram Well, in a sense. Mr Crabbe was, in fact, expecting Mr Winthrop but I'm—er—I'm—er—here—er—um . . .

Mark Instead.

Tristram Sorry?

Mark Instead. You're here instead.

Tristram Yes. Sorry. Yes. I've got the things here, you see—for him. For Mr Crabbe. To be ready to be signed. (*He stops for breath*) Sorry, you were saying . . .

Mark No, I wasn't.

Tristram Oh, right, I thought you were.

Mark No.

Tristram Ah.

Elizabeth returns from the bathroom and sits at her dressing-table. During the following she writes the envelope for the note, folds the note and putting it inside, seals the envelope

Mark (*after a pause*) Who are you, by the way?

Tristram Oh. I'm Mr Watson. Mr T. Watson. Sorry, I meant to say. I've—running . . .

Mark You've been running?

Tristram Yes.

Mark Right. You'd better come in then, hadn't you? You can sit in here.

He ushers Tristram into the darkened sitting-room

Tristram Right, thanks. Thanks very much. I'm sorry to have . . .

Mark Mr Crabbe's not due for another half an hour. So you'd better make yourself at home. (*He starts up the stairs again*)

Tristram gropes across the darkened sitting-room, collides with the sofa and sits on it, clutching his briefcase. Mark goes into the bedroom. Elizabeth is sealing her note

Elizabeth Who was it?

Mark Someone from Speake, Tacket and Winthrop.

Elizabeth (*rising*) That's Roland's solicitors.

Mark Oh?

Elizabeth They're based in London. What are they doing here?

Mark There's only one of them.

Elizabeth Which one?

Mark I don't think he's absolutely sure himself. A Mr Watson.

Elizabeth I don't know a Mr Watson. What did he want? (*She places the note on the dressing-table*)

Mark Go and ask him. He's still down there.

Elizabeth You didn't let him in?

Mark I had to.

Elizabeth Oh really, Mark. Did you tell him I was here?

Mark Of course not.

Elizabeth Now, listen. I think I've got it all sorted out for us . . .

Mark I'm perfectly sorted out already, thank you.

Elizabeth You go and collect Kitty now, bring her back here and deliver

her and then run me straight to the station. Then you come straight
back here to Kitty and wait for Roland. All right?

Mark No.

Elizabeth Kitty can sleep upstairs in Mrs Ex-Awful P's old room. I'll
make the bed up for her. And I'll make you up a bed, if you insist on
sleeping apart, in the Dark Brown Room along the passage there.

Mark The Dark Brown Room?

Elizabeth It's the driest. I've slept in it once or twice. I can vouch for it.
Does that sound all right?

Mark It sounds dreadful.

Elizabeth It's a perfect solution. All you have to do is cancel that appalling
Bull Hotel place . . .

Mark And snuggle dcwn in the Dark Brown room . . .

Elizabeth Don't blame me. That's how they were decorated when we
moved in. You can take your pick of rooms if you want. There's the
Dark Brown, The Patchy Brown, The Mouldy Brown, The Nasty
Brown, The Dirty Brown and The Yucky-Awful-Foul Brown.

Mark Thanks. I'll stay at *The Bull*.

Elizabeth (*angrily*) My God, here I am, with my marriage in ruins,
breaking up around me even as I stand here and my own brother cannot
even be bothered to help. Well, I will tell you this, Mark. Neither you
nor anyone is going to stand between me and my freedom this time, do
you hear me? I'm warning you . . .

Mark What the hell are you talking about?

Elizabeth I won't let you stand between me and my career. I won't.

Mark (*thoroughly exasperated*) What do you mean?

Elizabeth Do you realize that I trained for ten years? Ten years of my
life so that I could dance. Why should I give that all up? For you or for
him.

Mark I'm not asking you to.

Elizabeth Look at this. (*She jetées across the room to Mark's amazement*)
Can you do that?

Mark It's very unlikely.

Tristram looks up at the ceiling at the thumping sounds above

Elizabeth (*swinging a leg high and on to the bed*) Or this?

Mark No.

Elizabeth (*slightly breathless from lack of practice*) Well then. (*She sits on
the stool*) And I'll tell you something. If you're not here when Roland
reads that note of mine, you can certainly say good-bye to any loan. If
you're here and very nice to him and hold his hand, then maybe.

Mark (*struck by this*) Really?

Elizabeth Certainly.

Mark Ah.

Elizabeth (*taking a key from the dressing-table drawer*) You'd better have
a spare front door key.

Mark takes it

Mark (*still unhappy at the arrangement*) O.K. Where are you staying when
    you get to London, anyway?
Elizabeth Maureen's.
Mark Which Maureen?
Elizabeth The Osterley Park Maureen.
Mark Oh, that Maureen. Enough said.
Elizabeth Go on.

Mark goes downstairs into the hall

   Elizabeth goes into the bathroom

Mark looks into the lounge where Tristram is still sitting in the dark

Mark All right, then?
Tristram Oh. Sorry. Yes, thank you.
Mark I'll be off now.
Tristram Yes.
Mark So there's er—there's nobody else at all in the house now.
Tristram No?
Mark No. Just you. So look after things.
Tristram Right. Yes. Well, I'll er—I won't . . .
Mark He shouldn't be long. 'Bye.
Tristram Good-bye—er—(*He rises and sits again*)

   Mark goes out the front door

*Tristram sits in the dark. After a second, he plucks up courage and switches
on the table lamp next to him. It does not appear to work. After a pause,
Tristram tries another lamp further away. That does not work either.*

Tristram sits again. He whistles to himself very quietly

   Upstairs, Elizabeth comes back from the bathroom

*Tristram hears her feet clomping across his ceiling. He stares up at it and
freezes, listening*

   *Elizabeth collects a fresh pair of tights from the dressing-table drawer and
   exits again to the bathroom*

*Tristram looks up again, startled. His whistling becomes a little more
agitated. He picks up a magazine and thumbs through it. Unable to see it, he
holds the magazine at arm's length and manages to read it with difficulty by
the light coming from the hall doorway. The front door opens. Tristram
replaces everything and sits expectantly*

   *Roland, a bucolic man in his forties, appears in the doorway, removing his
   hat*

Roland (*calling*) Darling. Lizzie girl. Darling . . . (*He hangs up his hat.
   Yelling in the direction of the kitchen*) Mrs P! I am back. Mrs P! (*He
   listens*)

   Elizabeth, upstairs, having heard something comes out of her bathroom and listens. When she hears nothing more, she shrugs and goes back in again

(*On getting no reply from the kitchen*) Oh well.

Roland goes into the lounge, switching on all the lights at the door as he does so. Tristram blinks in the light and stands up

Good Lord, who are you?

Tristram Hallo. I'm . . . Are you Mr Crabbe?

Roland I'm Crabbe, yes.

Tristram Sorry. I'm er—you see, Mr Winthrop . . .

Roland Mr Winthrop?

Tristram No, I'm not Mr Winthrop.

Roland Just a minute. I know who you are. Mr Curry phoned me from Mr Miller's. You're Mr Watson.

Tristram Yes.

Roland Splendid. I must apologize. I suddenly remembered twenty minutes too late that I'd agreed to meet here at six-fifteen. Have you brought everything?

Tristram Yes, yes. (*He waves his briefcase*)

Roland Good. First rate. Were you sitting in the dark for any reason or . . .

Tristram No, I was—er—just looking . . .

Roland Prefer to keep your coat, do you?

Tristram Er . . .

Roland Hang it up in the hall there.

Tristram (*getting up and removing his raincoat*) Right.

Roland What'll you drink?

Tristram (*going into the hall and hanging up his coat*) Er . . .

Roland Scotch, gin, vodka, Martini, you name it.

Roland goes into the study where the drinks are

Tristram Oh well, now then . . .

Roland (*off; not hearing him*) O.K. with Scotch, are you? Fine.

Roland comes back from the study and crosses the lounge to the hall

(*Yelling*) Mrs P! Where the hell is the woman? (*Bellowing*) Mrs P! Ice, please! Chop chop!

Upstairs, Elizabeth again appears at her bathroom door having thought she heard something. Hearing no more, she goes in again

Roland (*muttering, returning towards the study*) Place seems deserted.

Tristram Er—I think the house is no-one. But me in it . . .

Roland (*turning*) Pardon?

Tristram No-one but me. In it.

Roland Isn't there? How did you get in then?

Tristram Oh. Well, a man let me in.

Roland A man? What sort of man?

Tristram Oh, er—sort of that high . . . (*He indicates*)

Roland Well, where is he now?

Tristram He went out just before you came in.

Roland Curious. And you haven't seen my wife?

Tristram I don't think so.

Roland (*getting out some cigars*) If you'd seen my wife, you'd have remembered her, I can promise you that. And you didn't see a little, short, fat, dark woman—usually wearing glasses with her hair all over the shoot?

Tristram No. Is that Mrs Crabbe?

Roland The hell it's Mrs Crabbe. That's our Mrs Porter.

Tristram Ah.

Roland Who also seems to have disappeared. Do you mind it without ice?

Roland goes into the study

Tristram No, no.

Roland (*off*) Help yourself to a cigar.

Tristram Thank you. (*He does not*)

Roland (*off*) What ails Mr Winthrop, then?

Tristram I think he has a stomach.

Roland (*off*) A what?

Tristram Upset stomach. Upset.

Roland (*off*) Couldn't be bothered to make the journey himself, idle brute.

Tristram Well . . .

Roland (*off*) Or been on the booze again. Eh? If I know Basil Winthrop.

Tristram Ah.

Elizabeth returns from her bathroom, carrying a pair of freshly laundered pyjamas. She has changed into a dress. She clomps across to the bed, replaces her make-up bag in her handbag and puts her recently discarded skirt in the suitcase

Tristram, who has again heard her footsteps, stares up at the ceiling

Roland (*off*) How long have you been with Winthrop?

Tristram Well, only a matter of a few weeks, actually.

Roland (*off*) Office clerk, or something, are you?

Tristram No, I'm a junior partner.

Roland (*off*) Ah-ha.

Tristram Very junior.

Elizabeth leaves the master bedroom, carrying the pyjamas, and goes off along the first floor passage

Tristram glances up briefly

Roland returns bearing two very large Scotches and a soda siphon. He plonks the siphon on the table and hands Tristram a glass

Roland There y'are. Help yourself to that stuff if you want it. (*He nods at the siphon*) Personally I never touch it. (*He sits in the armchair*)

Tristram No, no, I won't either.

Roland Good man. Here's to you, sunbeam.

Tristram Yes. (*He raises his glass and drinks carefully*)

Elizabeth comes back along the first-floor passage, carrying clean sheets and a pillow-case. During the following, she goes upstairs to the attic bedroom

It's odd, you know, because although the man who—the man who let me in said the house was empty, but I keep thinking I hear someone upstairs. Footsteps. A woman's, I think.

Roland Ah well. Could be our ghost.

Tristram Really?

Roland Apparently, just after the place was built, the old boy who built it went bankrupt and had to sell it off cheaply. And he sold it to some woman and she turned it into a brothel, would you believe.

Elizabeth switches on the attic bedside table lamp

Tristram Good heavens.

Roland Right out here. Miles from anywhere much. Very exclusive apparently. Catering for well-to-do Victorian gentry and all that.

Tristram Ah.

Elizabeth sniffs the sheets that are already on, decides they really are not too bad and, during the following, makes up the existing bed

Roland That bit's certainly true. That's on record. Then apparently, legend has it, one of her girls gets into a fight with a client and he runs her through with his swordstick. Which wasn't very pleasant. She dies, naturally, there's a terrific scandal and the place is closed. Now, when it is eventually resold after ten years or so, there's this wretched girl, the one who's been murdered, still prowling around.

Tristram Goodness.

Elizabeth sits on the bed

Roland And if you're her type and she takes a fancy to you, apparently she's even been known to climb into bed with you. Being the sort of woman she was, eh? (*He laughs*)

Tristram laughs

Only trouble is, if she does take a shine to you, you'll be dead in the morning.

Tristram Ah.

Roland Extracting her revenge, I suppose. Exacting her revenge. Some people say exacting, I say extracting. Load of old rubbish really but still makes for a good story. Care for another?

Tristram Oh no . . .

Roland (*rising*) Hang on, I'll top you up. Save me going backwards and forwards.

Roland takes both glasses into the study to refill them

Elizabeth rises simultaneously, having finished in the attic. She turns off the light and comes down the attic stairs with the sheets and pillow-case. Tristram starts to unpack his own briefcase, spreading the documents on the table

Elizabeth goes off along the first-floor passage

Roland (*off*) You drive down?

Tristram No, I came on the train.

Roland (*off*) Staying over?

Tristram Yes, at the—*Bull*, I think it's called.

Roland (*off*) Really. You should have stayed at *The Boar's Head*. Much
better. Very good restaurant.

*Elizabeth returns from putting away the sheets and goes back in the master
bedroom*

*During the following, Tristram again hears her pass above him as she goes
to the bed and closes her cases*

Tristram Ah well, the firm's paying, of course.

Roland (*off*) Much cheaper at *The Bull*, mind you. Should be. All that
traffic rumbling past.

Tristram Yes.

Roland (*off*) You won't sleep a wink.

Roland returns with the glasses even fuller

Tristram Ah well.

Roland There y'are. (*He puts Tristram's glass down*)

Tristram Thank you.

Roland Food's lousy at *The Bull* as well. (*Settling down*) Well, what do you
think of this place? What you've seen of it in the dark?

Tristram Well . . .

Roland Probably think I'm a lunatic buying it, don't you?

Tristram No. No . . .

Roland Yes, you do. Yes, you do. Don't blame you. (*More confidentially*)
Listen. Business for just a second, right?

Tristram (*alert immediately*) Yes, yes.

Roland This Bainbridge man'll be here in a minute. (*Consulting his watch*)
I asked him to look in about—er . . .

Tristram This is the vendor?

Roland The man who's selling it. He'll be here in a second so let me fill you
in. First of all, I think I've definitely decided I'm going through with the
purchase of this place. We'll probably give him a bit of a dance first but
I think I've made up my mind.

Tristram I see, I see.

Roland The point is, you're absolutely right, of course. The place is totally
beyond the pale. But you see, Mr Watson, over and above a lot of
things I'm a great believer in family. That make any sense to you?

Tristram Oh yes. Your family are here, are they? From here?

Roland No, they're not.

Tristram Ah.

Roland It's my wife's family. They're the local people.

Tristram Oh, I see. You didn't want to live where you were brought up?

Roland I was brought up in Singapore.

Tristram Oh, I see.

Roland Which is a hell of a long way to commute on a Monday morning.

Tristram (*laughing*) Yes, yes.

Roland No, the point is, not wishing to bash around in the bushes, Mr Watson, I've made a great deal of money. A great deal of money.

Tristram Yes, yes.

Roland If you want to put it in those terms, I'm a successful man.

Tristram Yes.

Roland No, to hell with it. Why not say it? I'm a very successful man.

Tristram Right.

Roland And very successful men, let's be truthful about this, very successful men should live in very big houses. Am I right?

Tristram looks blank

Or am I not right?

Tristram (*scarcely following this logic*) Oh yes.

Roland Otherwise, there seems to me to be no point in being very successful, does there?

Tristram No.

Roland There you are. Wife's family district. Big houses. I look around and I come up with this place. *The Pines.* Miles from anywhere. Of course, nobody else wants it. I'm getting it for a song, you know.

Tristram Yes, well, of course I saw the . . .

Roland Needs masses doing to it, of course.

Tristram Yes.

Roland Now this Bainbridge chap when he comes. He's a local builder. I don't know how he got to own this place. Didn't ask. But I did give him the impression when I wrote to him that he might be the lad to do the improvements. He seemed pretty keen. So we'll sound him out there, as well. Now. Everything's clear on the legal side, is it?

Tristram (*clearing his throat*) Yes. We have only to cheque the payment—of the—no—pay the chequement of the vendor—of the—sorry. Of the purchaser. Outstanding. (*He clears his throat*)

Roland Pardon, I didn't quite . . .

Tristram Sorry. I've got the contractual finalizations—er—the finalized contractuals—rather, contracts—ready. So there should be no obvious—er—er—er—oh—er—constructions—er—obstructions. Right. To the payments and completion. Of it all. (*Pause*) Yes.

Roland (*after some thought*) Yes, I see. (*He studies Tristram*) Excuse me asking but you're going into this legal business full time, are you?

Tristram Yes.

Roland Ah-ha.

Tristram I am. In it.

Roland Full time?

Tristram Yes. Sorry, was there . . . ?

Roland No, no. It's just that—er—well, if you don't mind my saying so, yours doesn't immediately strike a layman like myself as what we generally think of as a legal brain. Just a first impression.

Tristram Well, yes. I'm more usually on the papers. Work. Paper.
Roland Oh, paper.
Tristram Yes.
Roland Ah well, there's masses of that, isn't there, in your business? You'll be all right there.
Tristram Yes.

A pause. They appear to have run out of conversation

Roland Fancy a peanut, do you?

Elizabeth returns from the master bathroom, now in her coat and ready to leave. She picks up her cases and moves to the bedroom door

Tristram Er ...
Roland Or an olive, perhaps? Yes, an olive. That'd be nice. (*Crossing to the hall door and shouting*) Mrs P! Mrs P! (*He listens*)

Elizabeth again stops as she reaches the bedroom door, believing she heard something. Hearing no more, she moves on

Sorry about this. It's really most odd. Can't think where she's ... (*Yelling*) Mrs P!

Elizabeth, half-way downstairs, freezes

Elizabeth (*to herself*) Oh, dear God.
Roland (*returning to the lounge*) Well, I'm sorry. I give up. Wait there. I may have the odd nut in the sideboard.

Roland goes into the study

The front doorbell rings. Elizabeth stands stock still, then slowly begins to back up the stairs again with her suitcases

(*Off*) That could be Bainbridge. Let him in, there's a good chap.
Tristram Right.

Tristram goes through the hall to the front door. Intent upon opening the door, he catches only a glimpse of Elizabeth out of the corner of his eye. He looks again but she has gone. He reassures himself with a little whistle. Elizabeth takes refuge off along the first-floor landing, still with her suitcases. Tristram opens the front door

Leslie is standing outside. He is a perky little man in his late thirties. He is difficult to recognize at all at present, as he is clad in full motor-cycle gear

Tristram steps back alarmed, with a cry

Leslie (*stepping smartly into the hall*) Good evening. Mr Crabbey, I presume?
Tristram No, I'm Mr Watson.
Leslie Mr Watson?
Tristram Yes, Mr Crabbe is ... (*He indicates the lounge*)
Leslie Oh, I see. I do beg your pardon. Leslie Bainbridge. How do you do?

Roland jumps up and down in the middle of the attic bedroom floor

(*As he does so*) See that? See what happens?

Leslie I think that's natural spring. It's all timber, you see. We're talking pre-steel R.S.J.s.

Roland You jump over there. I'll jump over here.

Leslie Right.

Leslie and Roland jump with a will. Tristram bounces up and down on his toes, as the floor vibrates

Roland You watch for the sag.

Leslie Yes, yes.

Roland (*continuing to bounce*) You see, there's definite bowing there. Just where Mr Watson's standing.

Tristram (*stepping rapidly back onto the landing*) Ah.

Leslie Could be. Could be you're right.

Roland (*ceasing to bounce, a little breathless*) Now, I don't like the look of that at all, Mr Bainbridge.

Leslie (*stopping, similarly breathless*) No, well, we'll have that up. We can have that up.

Roland We better had. Our room's under here. I don't want some housekeeper falling on top of me while I'm in bed. (*He turns off the bedside lamp*)

Leslie (*laughing*) No, that wouldn't do at all, would it?

Roland (*leading off again*) Right, down we go.

The three men go down the attic stairs

(*Consulting his notebook*) Now then, let's have a look at all these brown jobs along here.

Leslie Ah, you noted the linking colour schemes.

Roland You mean, all that brown there is your choice, is it?

Leslie Well my sister Pat must really take the credit. She wanted to achieve this autumnal feeling.

Roland (*going off along the landing*) She's certainly done that. It's like the Atacama desert along here.

Roland exits. Leslie follows him off

Tristram, alone, goes back into the master bedroom but sees no-one. Distantly is heard Leslie's laugh. Tristram starts to follow after them without much enthusiasm. The front door slams

Tristram scuttles off. Mark enters through the front door. He carries a small, new, blue suitcase

Mark (*to someone behind him*) Oh come on, Kitty, for heaven's sake. Do put your skates on.

Kitty, a rather cumbersome girl, in her late twenties, follows him in

(*Looking into the lounge*) Lizzie? Hallo? Anyone? No. (*To Kitty*) O.K. Look, I'll take you up. Follow on.

Mark marches up the main staircase. Kitty docilely follows

> (*As they go*) There's going to be a hell of a storm in a minute, isn't there? Glad we missed that.

They reach the first landing

> Just a tick, wait there.

Kitty waits obediently. Mark goes to the master-bedroom door

> Liz? Lizzie? (*He opens the door*) No. The note's still here so he isn't home either. (*He closes the door*) Right. Up we go again. Follow on.

Mark leads Kitty to the upper level

> (*As they go*) Bit of a turn up for the book, that, eh? Lizzie leaving Roland. I give up on her, I really do. Doesn't know what she does want half the time. (*Trying the attic bedroom light switch*) Damn. No bulb. Wait there. (*He gropes into the room*) Not the most elegant of rooms, this, but it's probably as good as you'd have got at *The Bull*. (*Discovering the table lamp*) Aha, what's this? (*He switches on the light*) There, O.K.?

Kitty nods

> You're looking absolutely awful, you know. You look as if you want a lot of food, a lot of fresh air and a lot of sleep. (*Picking up her suitcase again*) Oh, this is your case. I hung on to it. I had to. Your mother wouldn't take it back. I hope it's got everything you want. I haven't opened it. It's the one you—the one you were meaning to . . .

Kitty (*softly*) Yes, I know.

Mark Ah. (*He puts the case on the bed*) Listen, Kit, I'm in a bit of a rush. I'll be back as soon as I've got rid of Lizzie. The point is, as far as I'm concerned, it's square one, Kitty. I'm forgetting all that's happened over the past couple of months. It's like so much dirty water down the drain. You see? You're back home, that's all that matters to me, O.K.?

Kitty (*sitting on the bed*) Yes. (*As Mark speaks, her head slumps on to her chest*)

Mark That sort of life isn't for you, Kitty. Dancing about in the middle of Haverstock Hill. Your life's here, you see. With real people. Like me. Leave all that sort of behaviour to the people on TV. They get paid for it. You don't. So. Anyway. I think I'm very near landing that loan from Roland, if Lizzie doesn't upset the cart. Then I'm going to jack in this job at Foxton's. It's my view there isn't a lot of future in Personnel anyway—and we'll get that shop started. Between us. To begin with, I'm going to concentrate on purely fishing. Now, if that all works out, we might well branch off into guns. The whole thing really rests on whether I can . . . (*He tails off*) Kitty?

Kitty snorts awake

> Were you asleep?

Kitty I'm sorry. I'm very tired.

Roland Going to need my cheque book, aren't we?
Leslie I'm afraid so.
Roland I'll fetch it in a minute.

Thunder. A drop of rain from the ceiling hits Kitty. She sits up. Under the next, she hunts for a container to catch the drips. Eventually she finds a bucket in the cupboard

Hark at that.
Leslie Yes.
Roland Come in the car, I hope?
Leslie No. On the motorbike.
Roland Take your life in your hands with those. (*To Tristram*) Your car's here, I hope.
Tristram No, I walked up.
Roland What, from *The Bull*?
Tristram Yes.
Roland Athletic type, eh? He's staying at *The Bull*, this chap.
Leslie Oh, that's nice.
Tristram Yes?
Leslie They have excellent food there, too. Mrs Grout. Mention my name.
Tristram Right.
Leslie Les Bainbridge.
Tristram I will.
Leslie You'll get double portions.
Tristram Right, thank you.

Thunder. Kitty places the bucket under the drip. She sits on the bed, deep in thought

Roland I'd give you a lift back down there, only I don't drive in the evenings if I can help it. The police in these parts can be very, very sticky. I've been stopped on countless occasions for absolutely no reason. (*Draining his glass*) I don't know about you, I'm going to have one more for the road and then I'm going to start sending search parties out for my wife.
Tristram There's the note here. I don't know if . . .
Roland What's that?
Tristram This note.
Roland Oh good lord, there's the note. We'd all forgotten the note, hadn't we? Let's have a look at this note. (*He starts to open it*) Let's read her excuses, shall we?

The phone rings in the study. Kitty stands up. She has come to a decision. She puts down her nightdress and rummages in her suitcase until she finds her sponge-bag

Kitty goes off into the bathroom with her sponge-bag

Roland, meanwhile, moves towards the study to answer the telephone. He tosses the note on to the table so that it lands nearer to Leslie

What do you bet this'll be her? Tell you what, you read that note, I'll answer the phone. We'll see if her story tallies.

Roland goes into the study

Leslie (*picking up the note*) Well, shall I solve the mystery?

Roland's voice is heard off, answering the telephone

Roland (*off*) Hallo. . . . Hallo, Reggie. Good to hear your voice. . . . Yes, it's Roly. Reggie, how's Penny?

Leslie Now then. (*Reading*) "My—darling—" oh, yes. Yes. (*He reads the note silently*)

Roland (*off*) Good, good. And Winnie? . . . Winnie's all right? . . . Splendid. Got over all that—er . . . Good. Listen, Reggie, Lizzie's not here at the moment. At a guess, she's either at Peggy's or Monty's . . . Yes. What can I . . .?

Leslie Oh dear.

Roland (*off*) Yes. What can . . .? Yes. . . . Yes. . . . What can I . . .? Yes. . . . Look, Reggie, just a tick. . . . Yes, just a trice.

Tristram (*over Roland's speech*) Pardon?

Leslie Oh dear.

Tristram What is it? What's the . . .

Leslie Oh dear. I think we may have problems here. (*He hands the note to Tristram*)

Roland appears round the door

Roland Excuse me just a tick. I've got Reggie Boggert on the line. I must have a quickie with him. By the way, what's she say?

Leslie Who's that?

Roland In the note. What does she say?

Leslie Ah, she says she's getting you a surprise but she'll be back shortly.

Tristram who is still ploughing through the note, looks up in amazement

Roland Oh, good show. Won't be a minute.

Roland goes back into the study and is heard to resume his conversation

Roland (*off*) Yes, Reggie, sorry. Back with you.

Tristram (*in a shocked undertone to Leslie*) Why did you say that?

Roland (*off*) I've got some people. Carry on, you were saying . . .

Tristram (*over this*) This doesn't—saying that.

Roland (*off*) Is that pounds or dollars? . . . Yes. . . . Yes. (*His voice fades away*)

Leslie Well, maybe not precisely.

Tristram Not remotely. It says she's leaving him.

Leslie Sssh, Mr Watson, please.

Tristram The man's wife is lefting him.

Leslie Mr Watson, may I say a few words?

Tristram But . . .

Leslie Please, Mr Watson.

Tristram What?

Leslie Now, I don't know if you're a family man, at all, Mr Watson.

Tristram Why?

Leslie I am. I am a big family man. I have huge responsibilities, Mr Watson. Mouths to feed. You follow me?

Tristram Yes.

Leslie Now, since my father, Bill, dear old Bill, retired from the firm, well, he was the image, if you follow me and the firm suffered. I suppose like everything else has these days. The little businesses struggling to make ends meet . . .

Tristram But what's this got to do with . . .?

Leslie I'm talking about kiddies, Mr Watson. Youngsters. Old folk. Pensioners. You follow me?

Tristram I don't know what you're talking about.

Leslie If I don't make this sale, if that cheque is not forthcoming, Bainbridge's goes to the wall, Mr Watson. That's my dilemma.

Tristram Ah.

Leslie Now you get the picture.

Roland, in the study, is heard laughing

Tristram But he's unlikely to sign once he's read this, is he?

Leslie Quite so.

Tristram Well.

Leslie There are kiddies involved here, Mr Watson.

Tristram Yes, you don't have to keep—have to keep telling me.

Leslie What I am asking is simply for five minutes of your silence.

Tristram But I'm supposed—I mean as his legal—I'm not. I wouldn't. No. It's not—it isn't, really—I'm sorry. No.

Leslie Very well, Mr Watson. All I can say to you is, there will be hardship. Great hardship.

Tristram But surely I . . . (*In a great quandary*) Oh. Particularly.

Roland returns from his telephone call with a replenished glass and his cheque book

Tristram, in a rather reflex action, tucks the note he is holding, under his cushion

Roland Do you know, that was Reggie Boggert. I haven't seen or heard from Reggie Boggert, well . . . (*He tosses a cheque book on to the table*) Cheque book. (*Sitting in his armchair*) Right now. Oh, listen chaps, I'm afraid there's some rather grim news.

Leslie What?

Roland We appear to be running out of Scotch.

Leslie Well, that won't really worry me, Mr Crabbe, because I really must be hurrying along as soon as we've finished our business. Perhaps I should leave you and Mr Watson here for a moment to talk over the details. Eh, Mr Watson?

Tristram I'm—er—I . . .

Roland Fair enough.

Leslie If you'll excuse me, I'll just get kitted up then, ready to brave the elements.

Roland Surely.

Leslie (*going out to the hall for his gear*) Righty-ho. (*During the following he puts on his gear*)

Roland Jolly good. (*Confidentially to Tristram*) He's a thoroughly unpleasant little shit, isn't he? I mean, I don't take an instant dislike to anyone, you can't afford to in business but I certainly don't care for him. What do you think of him?

Tristram I don't know really, I . . .

Roland Righto, let's have a look at all this gubbins then. Sling it over.

Tristram Right. Here we are. This first.

Roland (*muttering through the text*) "This agreement, dated this—neeeurr-neeeurr-neeeurr—notwithstanding—neeeur-neeeur—" this is all standard, isn't it?

Tristram Yes, I think so.

Roland You think so? You're not very certain about a lot of things, are you, Mr Watson?

Tristram Er—no . . .

Roland No.

Tristram I don't think I can be.

Roland Not the best quality for a lawyer. Pen, pen.

Tristram Here. (*He produces a pen*)

Roland Well, now. Come on then. Before I sign these, give me one firm opinion. I won't necessarily take it but I'd like to hear you give one just once. Now then, do you personally think I ought to buy this place, yes or no?

Tristram Er . . .

Roland No "er". Yes or no.

Tristram No.

Roland No?

Tristram No.

Roland Why not?

Tristram Er . . .

Roland Too pricey?

Tristram No.

Roland Needs too much doing to it? Wrong neighbourhood? What then?

Tristram Well. (*Producing Elizabeth's note from under the cushion*) This.

Roland What's that?

Tristram It's a note from your wife.

Roland What? Back soon with a big surprise, that note?

Tristram Yes. Only not that note. I mean, that's not what it says.

Roland What does it say, for heaven's sake?

Tristram It's meant for you. (*He hands Roland the note*)

Roland "My darling, Maybe this letter—neeeur-neeeur—surprise after all. Quite simply—neeeur-neeeur—gone. As you—neeeur—neeeur—carnage—neeeur—neeeur . . ."

Tristram watches him. At length, Roland folds up the note and puts it into his pocket

(*After a bit*) Yes. Well, I must say that's a—that certainly puts a new . . . (*He tails away*)

Tristram watches him uneasily. Suddenly, Roland starts crying: a series of awful, shuddering sobs. Tristram is transfixed in horror. Leslie returns in his motor-cycle gear, carrying his crash helmet

Leslie What's wrong with him?

Tristram He's—er. . . .

Leslie He was all right a minute ago. What've you done to him?

Tristram He read the—he read the note.

Leslie (*urgently*) But did he sign first?

Tristram No.

Leslie (*with a gesture of frustration*) Oh, damn it. Damn it. I beg your pardon, but damn it.

Roland (*through his tears*) I really must apologize—I'm making an absolute . . . I really must apologize.

Leslie No, quite understandable. Don't mind me. I'm just off anyway.

Roland I knew she'd do this. I knew it would happen. It's happened before, you see.

Tristram With your wife?

Roland You can't trust any of them.

Tristram She's left you before?

Roland No, no, not this one. My other wife. I've had three. I buried one and lost two.

Leslie Oh, dear. (*He starts to put on his crash helmet and gauntlets*)

Roland (*to Tristram*) It's not fair, you know. It's not as if I was the sort of chap to go polly-arsing around, you know, chasing after women. She couldn't have asked for a more . . . You know what they were saying to her at our wedding? Everybody in that miserable, rancid little registry office was saying: "You're a damned lucky woman, Mrs Crabbe. You're damned lucky to get him." The registrar, he said it. I'll tell you who else said it. That fellow, Andrew Thingummytyke said it. And he doesn't say these things off the top of his head. He's a judge. He can't afford to make these sort of statements.

Tristram I think he's delirious.

Leslie Mr Crabbe? Mr Crabbe?

Roland (*seeing Leslie in his full gear for the first time*) My God, who are you?

Leslie Leslie Bainbridge, Mr Crabbe.

Roland You look like the Angel of Death.

Leslie Yes, that's right. (*To Tristram*) I'll pop in first thing tomorrow and see how things are. Just in case he's feeling a little more like—er—you know, in the cold light of morn. (*He removes his helmet*)

Roland (*over this*) That's it, isn't it? That's the end of it. That's curtains.

Tristram We can't leave him like this. Can you at least hand him upstairs. With me? Please? He's gone an improbable colour.

Roland resumes sobbing

Leslie Well . . . (*He moves back*)

Tristram Mr Crabbe, I wonder if you'd lie down. Whether you'd like a lie. Mr Crabbe . . .

Roland Bloody women. Never trust them. Never. They take you for what they can get out of you.

Tristram Take his other arm, would you, Mr . . .

Roland (*as they help him up*) Whadya doing?

Leslie Upsadaisy, then.

Roland Thank your lucky stars you're not a woman, matey.

Leslie No, sorry, afraid not. . . .

Roland Or I'd punch you right in the eye.

Tristram Upstairs now.

Tristram and Leslie take Roland towards the stairs.

Roland You wouldn't credit it, would you? Everything's shared. I said to her, "With practically all my worldly goods I do thee endow, pretty nearly. They're all yours." And you know what she said?

Tristram No, what did she say?

Roland She said, "Everything"—this is funny, this is—she said, "everything I have is yours." Only difference was she didn't have anything. Little, frigid, knock-kneed, telly commercial go-go dancer with a giro account in Swindon. I don't call that a dowry, do you?

Leslie No, no.

There is a clap of thunder. The trio climb to the top of the main stairs

Kitty returns from the attic bedroom with her sponge-bag, which she puts back in her suitcase. During the following, she takes a writing pad from the case and starts to write a note

Roland Do you know something interesting? The whole time I've lived with that woman, I have never seen her scratch herself. Not once. I'd call that unnatural, wouldn't you? Grounds for divorce, don't you think so, Mr Watson? Failure to itch.

Tristram Rather.

They reach the master bedroom

(*To Leslie*) This is his room, isn't it?

Leslie Master bedroom, yes.

Roland (*at the bed*) Where are we? In the Bridal Suite, are we? (*He laughs*) Do you get that? Bridal Suite.

Leslie (*as they lay him on the bed*) Yes, yes. Here we are, then. You'll feel better in the morning.

Tristram (*to Leslie, as he loosens Roland's collar*) Take his shoes off, will you?

Roland (*while they minister to him*) Do you know how much this mattress cost me? This orthopaedic mattress? Purchased at her institution. Instigation. Some people say instigation, I say institution. It's supposed

Mark below him, hears the rapping and stares up at the ceiling suspiciously

(*Continuing*) Dot, dot, dot. Dash, dash, dash. Oh this is hopeless. Dot, dot, dot.

Mark (*his eyes narrowing*) Hang on. Dah, dah, dah. O. Dit, dit, dit. S. Dah, dah, dah. O.S.O. Odd. (*Trying it out*) Ohso, Osso? Ozzo? (*Realizing*) Oh! Heavens! (*He bounds up from his chair, across the hall and up the stairs to the master bedroom door. Knocking softly but insistently*) Roland? Roly, are you all right?

Tristram (*in a whispered shout*) Help.

Mark Roly?

Tristram (*as before*) Help, help.

Mark opens the door cautiously

Mark Roly?

Tristram (*still sotto voce*) Please help me.

Mark What?

Tristram Help, could you please?

Mark What the . . . ?

Tristram Sssh.

Mark What the hell is going on?

Tristram It's all right, I've worked it out. My life isn't in danger until the sun catches the pillow.

Mark Have you an explanation for all this?

Tristram Not really. I think it's to do with the paranormal laws of the supernatural.

Mark The what?

Tristram It's something we're barely beginning to understand.

Mark You're absolutely right. Not one word. Who are you?

Tristram I'm Mr . . . I'm Tristram Speake and Watson. No, just Watson.

Mark What?

Tristram Watson. I'm Watson.

Mark Yes, of course. I remember you from last night. What are you doing here?

Tristram I'm here for Mr Crabbe. I'm soliciting for Mr Crabbe.

Mark (*arching his eyebrows*) Are you indeed?

Tristram Yes. Hallo again.

Mark Then what are you doing in bed with that lady?

Tristram (*excitedly*) Then you can see her too, then? She's also visible to you, is she?

Mark Of course she's visible to me. There's about one hundred and twenty pounds of woman in that bed. What do you think I am, an idiot? I repeat, what are you doing in bed with Mrs Crabbe?

Tristram I was—I was . . . Mrs Crabbe? Mrs . . . ? Thissy Missy Crabbe? Crabbey Miss . . . is it?

Mark (*contemptuously*) You know damn well it is, you little swine. And for your information, she also happens to be my sister.

Tristram Your sissy missy . . . ?

Mark (*fiercely*) Now, keep your voice down. Perhaps you'd be so good as to step out on to the landing.

Tristram Yes, right. Sorry, yes.

Mark I'll be waiting for you. And don't wake her up. There's no point in embarrassing her needlessly.

Tristram No. Sorry.

Mark starts to leave. Tristram struggles to get free from Elizabeth's grip. As he battles, she stirs

(*Calling in a low whisper*) I say, excuse me, Mr—I say . . .

Mark (*coming back*) What?

Tristram Could you possibly lend a hand. I'm frightened I'll wake her, you see.

Mark (*coming closer*) What?

Tristram Could you lever her apart? Like that? And I'll slide out.

Mark Yes, all right.

Mark forces Elizabeth's hands apart with difficulty. Tristram slips out from her grip and slithers to the floor. Deftly, he replaces himself with a pillow. Mark releases Elizabeth's arms and they clamp back around the pillow, crushing it. Mark covers her with the duvet

Wow!

Tristram She's very strong.

Mark She's a dancer.

Tristram (*making an attempt at a joke*) She must dance on her hands.

Mark (*crushingly*) Kindly step out on to the landing, please.

Tristram Certainly. Sorry.

He follows Mark on to the first floor landing

Mark (*when they are alone*) All right. Now, I'm a fair man. I ought by rights to be phoning the police this very minute and having you charged with everything from breaking and entering through to statutory rape. But before I do so, I am prepared to listen to your side. To be quite frank with you, I don't believe for a minute that you're going to be able to come up with any explanation that will satisfy me but you're free to try. So go ahead. Say your piece.

Tristram (*taking a deep breath*) Well. It's very simple. Quite simply, I am on a Winthrop. On Mr Winthop's, sorry. Behalf of him. For the completion of Mr Crabbe. And yesterday evening, we were going to be exchanging Mr Bainbridge. For contracts already drawn. And then, along came Mrs Crabbe's note. And after it was discovered. *The Bull* was cancelled you see. I think, because of the embrocation really. Sounds silly. And so Mr Crabbe went up and I stayed down instead. And then came all this Scarlet Lucy business and it was a pure mistake. Honestly. In a nutshell.

Mark (*after a pause*) Well, I'll say this for you. You're a pretty plausible devil. I suspect if one examined it in detail, that story wouldn't hang together for a second but somehow I don't think you're clever enough

have lived to regret for the rest of your life. It's not worth it, old man, believe me. Not just because a woman leaves you. And, my God, you're talking to someone who's really been left, you know. If you want to know about leaving people, you talk to me. I don't understand what got in to her, really. I still don't, to this day. (*He sits down on a chair, absorbed again in his own problems and forgetting Roland*) Sometimes I look back to see if there was some clue in her behaviour that I missed.

Roland starts to snore gently

Something that should have said to me: watch it, old son, she'll be leaving you pretty soon. But there was nothing. Nothing at all. We always seemed to hit it off, you see, that was the odd thing.

Tristram arrives back

We never quarrelled, we never had an angry word between us. We . . .
Tristram You've let him go to sleep.
Mark Oh, hell. (*Shaking Roland*) Roly! Roly! I was talking to him, too, I don't know how it happened.

Mark shakes Roland again, but Roland only groans

He's absolutely flat out now. He's going—we're losing him. I know. Sing.
Tristram What?
Mark Sing, man, sing. (*Singing*) For he's a jolly good fellow.

Tristram joins in with him, putting down the packet of glucose tablets and the vitamin pills he has been carrying

Tristram⎫ For he's a jolly good fellow, for he's a jolly ⎫
Mark　　⎭ good fellow and so say all of us.　　　　　　 ⎬ (*Singing together*)
　　　　　　　　　　　　　　　　　　　　　　　　　 ⎭

They cheer and clap. Elizabeth during this, sits up in bed wide awake. She glares at the floor from whence this noise emanates

Elizabeth Oh, for heaven's sake! What on earth . . .?

Elizabeth gets out of bed and goes into the master bathroom and, in a moment or so, returns wearing her dressing-gown and slippers

Roland, still half asleep, acknowledges the singing and applause. He rises

Roland Thank you. Thank you.
Mark That's done the trick, he's talking again.
Roland Thank you very much indeed.
Tristram We'll have to keep noising at him.
Roland Now, it's at about this time every year that we, the management, like to come along and have a chat to you fellows there on the shop floor.
Tristram What's he talking about?
Mark It doesn't matter, he's talking.

They applaud again. Roland acknowledges this. Elizabeth comes downstairs

Roland Now, I'm sure it's true that every single one of you chaps must at some time—probably just as you're completing your hundredth bucket of the day, must have stopped and wondered what it's all about. And it's a perfectly natural question to ask oneself. What's in all this bucket business for me? Well, I can answer that in one phrase. Like everything else in this world, there is in buckets what you personally choose to put in them . . .

More applause from Mark and Tristram. Roland sits. Elizabeth arrives in the doorway in her dressing-gown and slippers

Elizabeth What on earth is going on?

Mark and Tristram spring up

Mark Ah.
Tristram Oh.
Elizabeth Roland? Roly?
Roland So . . . (*Seeing her through bleary eyes*) Hallo, it's Lizzie. It's my little Lizzie. Hallo, Lizzie, welcome aboard.
Elizabeth He can't be drunk, now.
Mark He's not, he's . . .
Tristram He's . . .
Elizabeth Who are you?
Tristram I'm—er—Mr . . . Hallo again.
Elizabeth We haven't met before, have we?
Mark No.
Tristram No. Watson.
Mark Mr Watson. He's from Speake and Whosit.
Elizabeth And what's the matter with Roly?
Mark Well, he's—er . . .
Tristram He's asleep.
Elizabeth I can see that. But he's dead on his feet. What's happened to him?
Tristram He—took a few.
Elizabeth (*sharply*) What?
Tristram He took—some things, you see. To help him forget about—about Mrs Crabbe. You. And he didn't know his own strength. And so he, you see, he—well, he . . .
Elizabeth Oh, shut up.
Tristram Sorry.
Elizabeth Mark.
Mark Hallo.
Elizabeth I want an explanation, Mark. Why has my husband been dragged down here while he's still asleep? And why are you both down here singing and shouting at him at seven in the morning?
Mark Well, you see, Lizzie, it's—er . . .
Elizabeth I'm a dancer, Mark, surely I don't have to remind you. And a dancer needs sleep. Or she can't work.
Mark Quite, quite.

Tristram Well, that applies to . . .

Elizabeth Shut up! (*To Mark*) Well?

Mark Yes. O.K. Well. Brace yourself. Roly tried to kill himself.

Elizabeth (*slight pause*) Roly?

Mark Yes.

Elizabeth Oh, no.

Mark Easy—easy . . .

Elizabeth Because of me?

Mark So far as we can gather.

Elizabeth Oh. Oh—how little we know people.

Mark Yes—well . . .

Elizabeth And I thought he'd forgiven me. How did it happen?

Mark You really want to know?

Elizabeth Yes.

Mark Piecing it together, it seems he went upstairs to sleep in the attic room last night, taking some sleeping-tablets with him . . .

Elizabeth Mine probably.

Mark Yes, I think they were. Then he lay down on the bed up there, wrote a little note: this life isn't for me any longer . . .

Elizabeth Is that what it said?

Mark Roughly. Then in the morning, we—I went up to see if Kitty was O.K.—that's it. I think he's going to turn the corner though, Lizzie.

Elizabeth (*going to Mark and clinging to him*) Oh, Mark . . .

Mark (*holding her*) I'm sorry.

A silence. Tristram looks away, trying not to intrude upon this touching scene

Elizabeth You said he went up to the attic room last night?

Mark Yes.

Elizabeth He couldn't have done.

Mark Eh?

Elizabeth He was in bed with me, certainly till the early hours.

Mark Oh. Are you sure?

Elizabeth Yes. As a matter of fact, I am. Very.

Mark Ah.

Elizabeth So. He couldn't have gone up to the attic last night, could he?

Mark Suppose not.

Elizabeth So somebody's lying.

Mark No.

Elizabeth If he was in bed with me till the small hours, then he certainly wasn't in the attic. He could have gone up to the attic after he'd been in bed with me and taken the pills then and written the note . . .

Mark Yes, yes. That's probably what . . .

Elizabeth But then that doesn't tally with your story that you saw him going upstairs last night.

Mark Hang on, hang on. What about this? Perhaps. This is perhapsing. Perhaps he went up to bed in the attic last night, took the pills, wrote the note and went to bed. Then he heard you coming to bed so he came downstairs and he got into bed with you. Then after he'd been with you—(*slowing up*)—he got out again afterwards—this isn't really holding together, is it?

Elizabeth No.

Mark No.

Elizabeth Of course, the other alternative is that it wasn't him at all.

Mark In the attic.

Elizabeth In bed with me.

Mark Hah. Oh well, that's pretty remote, isn't it?

Elizabeth But somebody else.

Mark Yes, yes.

Elizabeth And it was somebody else, wasn't it?

Mark Er—well . . .

Elizabeth Who was it, Mark?

Mark Er . . .

Tristram Me.

Elizabeth You?

Tristram Yes. Hallo again.

Elizabeth I see. I won't ask what you were doing in my bed or why you said nothing when I got in with you.

Tristram Well, it was—er . . . I thought you were somebody else.

Elizabeth (*coolly*) Anyone in particular?

Tristram Er . . .

Mark (*fidgeting uneasily*) Look, Lizzie, this is really desperately embarrassing. I mean, if you insist on talking about it . . .

Elizabeth I most certainly do. My God, I spent a night with this man, this is the first time I've seen his face.

Tristram smiles at her

Mark Well then, may I suggest if you want to discuss it, it might be better if you left the room.

Elizabeth Then how can I discuss it?

Mark Well then, Mr Watson should leave the room.

Elizabeth What's the point of that?

Mark Well, somebody's got to leave the room, for heaven's sake. This is very embarrassing.

Elizabeth Why don't you leave the room?

Mark (*indicating Tristram*) I'm not leaving you with him.

Elizabeth It's all right, Roland's here.

Mark Just about.

Elizabeth You realize, Mr Watson, that you have put my marriage at risk?

Tristram Ah, yes. Sorry.

Elizabeth When my husband finds out about this, which he will do, make no mistake, things are going to become very unpleasant. For all of us.

Tristram Really?

Elizabeth My husband is devoted to me, you see. It would not be going too far to say that he worships me. Did you know I was a dancer, Mr Watson?

Tristram Yes, go-go, yes.

Elizabeth I beg your pardon.

Tristram Sorry.

Elizabeth My husband caught his first glimpse of me dancing. It was that image he fell in love with, I'm afraid. The ephemeral, the graceful. Of course, it's not really like that at all. It's years of training and sacrifice, endless workouts, the hard day-in, day-out, physical grind. Dancing is sweat, Mr Watson. Not lady-like perspiration but basic, God-given sweat. Tortured lungs and aching muscles.

Tristram (*riveted*) Yes, yes.

Elizabeth My husband doesn't understand that. Why should he? Like the rest of the general public, all he really wants to see is the tinsel.

Tristram Ah. Yes, that sounds all very possible.

Elizabeth Mr Watson, I'm going to have to ask you to leave this house. Now. Do you mind?

Tristram (*rising*) No, not at all.

Elizabeth You understand?

Tristram Yes.

Elizabeth Do you have any clothes?

Tristram Er, yes—they're in the—in the bathroom.

Elizabeth My bathroom?

Tristram In the airing cupboard.

Elizabeth Well, will you take them out and find somewhere other to put them on, please.

Tristram Yes. Yes, of course. Sorry. (*He goes to the door*)

Mark And get a move on.

Tristram Right.

Tristram goes up the main staircase, into the master bedroom and through into the master bathroom

Roland breathes on heavily

Mark Lizzie, I'm shattered to hear all this, really. I'm so sorry. It must have been a ghastly experience.

Elizabeth No.

Mark No.

Roland snores

Elizabeth Could you do something about Roland's breathing, please? Try tilting his head, it sometimes helps.

Mark Will do. (*He tips Roland's head the other way*)

Elizabeth Do you know where my sleeping-pills have got to? I think I'd better take a couple now, as well.

Mark (*looking round and seeing them on the side table*) Er—yes, they're on here. With the . . .

Elizabeth What's that?

Mark It's Roland's farewell note. Do you want to . . .?

Elizabeth No, not now . . .

Mark No, it's rather pathetic.

Elizabeth I couldn't now. Just leave it there.

Mark (*putting it on the table in front of her with the pills*) Do you want some water with these?

Elizabeth Yes, pour me a tonic water, will you? I'll have that.

Mark Certainly.

Mark goes into the study

Elizabeth takes the last two tablets from her bottle

Elizabeth I must get some more of these.

From the master bathroom comes the sound of a running tap and Tristram gargling again. The tank above Kitty begins to refill. She bangs her cupboard door helplessly

Kitty Oh . . .

Mark returns with a glass of tonic water

Mark Here.

Elizabeth Thank you. (*She takes her pills*)

Mark Actually, Lizzie, something rather worrying's happened.

Elizabeth Mmm?

Mark Kitty's taken off again. I put her to bed in the attic bedroom last night. . . .

Elizabeth What, the one Roland was in?

Mark Yes.

Elizabeth How many people were in there?

Mark That's the mystery. I don't know. Certainly not Kitty. She's vanished again. She's left her suitcase—mind you, she usually does that. You see, Lizzie, I know you've got problems of your own but—Kitty obviously needs taking in hand. Everyone's agreed on that. I mean, she's a chaotic character. She's no sense of direction whatever. She needs managing, if you like. Sorting out. Putting on the rails. Telling what to do. But the trouble is, whenever I do try to sort her out, she refuses to be sorted. So what can I do? I ask you . . .

Mark sees Elizabeth is asleep, breathing deeply. Roland snores. Kitty, in her cupboard, snores

Oh. O.K. I'll have a bath and get dressed then.

Mark leaves Roland and Elizabeth in the lounge sleeping peacefully. Between them, on the table, lie Kitty's note and the bottle of pills, now empty and unstoppered. Mark goes up to the first floor landing

Tristram comes out of the master bedroom, carrying his clothes and his briefcase

What are you doing?

Tristram I was looking for somewhere to get dressed.
Mark Well, you can't have my room. Go upstairs.
Tristram Oh, yes, right, sorry.

Tristram goes upstairs to the attic bedroom

Mark goes along to the dark brown room

Tristram, in the attic bedroom, lays his clothes on the bed. Kitty pushes her cupboard door with a weary groan of misery. Tristram stops what he is doing and listens. Kitty pushes the door again and groans. Tristram locates the sound. Cautiously, he pulls the bed away from the cupboard door. Kitty, hearing him do this, crouches alert, ready for trouble, very apprehensive. Tristram sidles up, opens the cupboard door with a swift movement and steps back again, concealing himself. Kitty waits, not to be lured out. A pause. Tristram bounds round the door. Kitty jumps up, bangs her head on the tank and shouts. Tristram jumps back

Kitty What are you . . . ? What are you . . . ? What are you . . . ?
Tristram Now—now—I don't—I never . . .
Kitty Don't you—don't you—you . . .
Tristram I have absolutely none.
Kitty Oh?
Tristram So. Just you.
Kitty What?
Tristram Either.
Kitty All right.
Tristram Quite.

They look at each other for a second

Who are you? Who? Eh?
Kitty Never you—never you—I'm not. So there, as it happens. And if you—just you try it. And see if my fiancé will . . . Go ahead. Yes. See?
Tristram (*very puzzled*) What are you talking about?
Kitty If it comes. I could very well. Who are, in that case—who are— who are—who are—who are—who are—who are—who are—oh, bugger it. I can't—get it—who—who are . . .
Tristram (*simultaneously with her, slowly and carefully*)—Who—are—you?
Kitty Yes. Thank you.
Tristram I'm named Mr Watson.
Kitty Oh.
Tristram Tristram Watson. I'm Mr Crabbe's sort of solicitor.
Kitty I see. Well, you shouldn't go—you shouldn't . . . Be more careful.
Tristram Sorry.
Kitty Yes, well.
Tristram Sorry.
Kitty So. (*Pause*) Sorry.
Tristram Why were you in that cupboard?
Kitty I got stuck.
Tristram Oh. Bad luck.
Kitty Yes.

Tristram Often happens to me.

Kitty Does it?

Tristram Oh yes, often. (*Magnanimously*) Sit down.

Kitty Thank you. (*She does so, on the bed*)

Tristram I'll change elsewhere. Good morning. (*He picks up his clothes and goes to the door*)

Kitty Please . . .

Tristram (*turning*) Yes.

Kitty Could you—help?

Tristram Help?

Kitty I'm running away.

Tristram Are you? Why?

Kitty Oh. It's, well, my fiancé.

Tristram Mr . . .? Are you running from him, then?

Kitty No. Well. Partly. Yes. Mostly.

Tristram Oh. What's wrong with him?

Kitty Oh, he keeps—he keeps wanting things.

Tristram Ah.

Kitty No, I wouldn't mind *that*. Organizing things. Weddings and fishing shops and things.

Tristram Fishing shops.

Kitty Yes. You see, the trouble is when you don't know what it is you want to do with your life, people, they don't mean to, they make you feel guilty. And they make you feel you *should* know. And then they keep suggesting things. And you do feel guilty if you *don't* accept their suggestions. Because you have no suggestions yourself at all. The only thing you know definitely is that you don't want to do what they want you to do. But everything you do want to do, you haven't found out yet. Do you see?

Tristram Yes, I think I see that.

Kitty So. (*Pause*) I've never told anyone that before.

Tristram No? Your problem—your problem is . . .

Kitty What?

Tristram Well, it's not really your problem. You see, the way I see it, there are these people in the world who know what they're doing and what they want to do and what they want other people to do and they expect everyone else to join in or else.

Kitty Yes, yes.

Tristram And I think that we should all have the right not to do anything at all, if we don't want to. And if someone doesn't want to move a muscle ever again and it doesn't do any harm to anyone else, you should leave him sitting there and mind your own business. There's too many organizations and helpful suggestions and the sooner people are allowed not to do things the better. If you don't want to get married in a fishing shop, don't you. Sit down for your rights. And don't let anyone start organizing you or changing you because you're fine the way you are. Because who ever did make you did a bloody good job. There. Sorry, I'm terribly tired. May I sit down?

Kitty (*looking at him with some admiration*) Of course.
Tristram (*sitting beside her*) This is a nice bed. Better than the one downstairs.
Kitty Which one's that?
Tristram Oh, just the one I was sleeping in. Very treacherous. You've got a particularly nice face.
Kitty Really?
Tristram Yes.
Kitty So've—so've—so've . . .
Tristram So've I.
Kitty Yes.
Tristram Thanks. People do say it's a bit vacuous. Mr Winthrop, that's my boss, he calls me gormless.
Kitty You don't look gormless.
Tristram No, I don't think I do. Possibly my haircut. (*He lies down*) Sorry, do you mind?
Kitty No. (*Making room beside her*) Why don't you . . . ?
Tristram Right. Thank you. (*Wriggling up the bed*) Sorry.
Kitty Sorry.
Tristram You warm enough?
Kitty Yes.
Tristram Good. I'm warm enough. I'm lovely and warm now. I haven't been so warm for years and years.

Tristram falls asleep. Kitty sits beside him thoughtfully, then, after a second or so, kicks off her shoes and swings her legs up on the bed to lie beside Tristram. In a minute or two, she is also asleep. In the lounge, Roland and Elizabeth are deep asleep. The front door bell rings. Pause. Nobody stirs. The sound of the key in the lock and the front door is opened

> *Leslie enters. He is in his full all-embracing motorcycle kit as before, and is putting away a large bunch of many keys*

Leslie Hallo. Hallo, there? Anyone home? (*He looks in the lounge*) Oh, good heavens. It must be Mrs Crabbe, if I'm not . . . Hallo, I'm sorry, Mr Crabbe, if I'm in any way . . . Hallo? Excuse me . . . (*He knocks to wake them. Neither stir*) That's odd. (*He picks up the tonic water glass. He picks up the sleeping pill bottle and discovers it is empty*) Oh. Oh, now . . . (*He picks up the note. He unfolds it and reads it*) Oh dear. Oh, now that is a . . . Oh, good gracious . . . (*Shaking Roland*) Mr—Mr Crabbe? Wake up, wake up.
Roland (*savagely, in his sleep*) Don't start all that again, for God's sake.

Leslie recoils

Leslie (*turning to Elizabeth*) Mrs Crabbe? Mrs Crabbe . . . (*He seizes her by the shoulders*)
Elizabeth (*asleep*) Whaaa . . . ?
Leslie Wake up. Come on. Will you wake up? You can't sleep now, Mrs Crabbe. You'll be sorry for this. You must wake up. Come along. Come along now.

Elizabeth (*opening her eyes*) What's going ...? What's going ...? Who are you?

Leslie Come on, wake up, will you. Wake up.

Elizabeth What are you ...? Please, no ...

Leslie Come on, come on.

Elizabeth Please don't—please don't hurt me. I'm a dancer. You mustn't injure me.

Leslie Will you wake up?

Elizabeth (*clinging on to Leslie*) No—no ...

Leslie Now, now, let go. Let go. It's all right ...

Elizabeth My jewellery is upstairs. Take my jewellery, it's upstairs. But don't hurt me. I need my body for my work, you see. Please. (*She grips him tighter*)

Leslie Now, you're hurting me. Please, please. (*Yelling*) Let go!

Elizabeth slips to the ground, dragging Leslie down with her

Elizabeth (*screaming*) No, no. Help me, Roly. Roly, please. No, please. Help! Help!

Roland (*waking up through all this*) What in the hell ...? (*Seeing them*) My God!

Elizabeth (*screaming*) Roly!

Leslie (*in pain*) Aaaghh!

Roland (*staggering to his feet*) Oh no, you don't. You get off her. You get off my wife. You bloody little Hell's Angel. (*He grabs Leslie from behind*)

Elizabeth That's it, Roly, get him. Get him.

Roland I'll teach you, you thug.

Roland manages to drag Leslie away sufficiently to allow Elizabeth to crawl away a little distance towards the door

Leslie Let go, let go.

Roland Oh no, you ...

Leslie Aaaghh!

Leslie's boots come off in Roland's hands. He staggers back and continues fighting with them for a second in the belief that Leslie is still in them

Roland Aaaah!

Leslie, free, starts crawling towards the door and Elizabeth. Roland sees this

Look out, Lizzie. Stop him.

Elizabeth catches Leslie's head between her legs and traps his crash helmet in a head scissors. He finishes face down into the carpet

Elizabeth There.

Leslie Aaaah.

Roland Well done, girl.

Leslie (*in some pain*) Grooo ...

Roland Hold him, Lizzie, hold him. I'll just ...

Elizabeth (*panting with effort, banging her knee with her hand to tighten her grip*) Yes—yes ...

Roland taps Leslie's leg with his hand Leslie bangs the carpet in submission

Roland Now, listen to me, boy. My wife is a trained dancer and she has extremely powerful legs. If you wriggle around any more, I shall give her the word and she'll break your neck, do you hear me? Now, lie still.

Leslie lies absolutely still

That's shut him up. I'll fetch help, Lizzie.

Elizabeth Please be quick . . .

Roland I will. We'll tie him up and call the police. (*He runs into the hall, calling*) Mark! Mark! (*Going up the stairs a little way*) Mark!

Mark (*from a distance*) Hallo?

Roland Can you come, please? This is an emergency.

Mark A what?

Roland An emergency.

Mark Right.

In the attic, Kitty opens her eye and hears this but decides it is not important and slumbers on

Roland (*going downstairs and opening the front door to look out*) I'll just check there's no more of them. They like to hunt in packs, you know, these fellows.

Leslie shifts uncomfortably

Elizabeth (*striking her knee*) Lie still, will you?!

Mark comes along the first-floor passageway doing up his dressing-gown

Mark Hallo.

Roland goes up the stairs to meet him

Mark What's the problem?

Roland We've got an intruder. He broke in and tried to attack us. I woke up and found him at Lizzie's throat.

Mark My God, where is he?

Roland Lizzie's got him.

Mark Lizzie?

Roland Come on, this way. He's nothing spectacular. Just one of these ton-up thugs. His bike's just out there, you see. (*He indicates through the front door*)

Mark Oh, yes. So it is. It's a Yamaha.

Roland (*leading the way into the lounge*) In here. Good girl. Behaving himself?

Elizabeth Yes.

Mark (*still at the front door*) That's funny.

Roland What?

Mark What's he look like?

Roland I don't know. We haven't unmasked him yet.

Elizabeth Oh, do come on, someone, please.

Mark It's just I recognize the Yamaha. Or what there is of it. Let's have a look at him. Let him go.

Elizabeth Certainly not.

Roland What are you talking about?

Mark It's just that I think Lizzie may have Mr Bainbridge between her legs.

Elizabeth Mr Bainbridge?

Mark Your landlord. I'm almost certain.

Elizabeth Oh, no.

Elizabeth releases Leslie and draws away. Leslie comes up gasping

Mark Hallo, yes, it is. Mr Bainbridge.

Leslie (*finding his breath*) Ah. It's Mr Boxer, isn't it? Good morning.

Mark Good morning, Mr Bainbridge.

Leslie Mr Crabbe.

Roland Yes, hallo there.

Leslie It's a better morning.

Roland Would you care to—get up and sit down, Mr Bainbridge?

Leslie Thank you, thank you. I will. (*He sits and takes off his helmet*)

Roland This is Mr Bainbridge, dear. You haven't met my wife, Elizabeth, have you?

Elizabeth How do you do?

Leslie No, I haven't yet had the pleasure. How do you do, Mrs Crabbe.

Roland Well, I'm sorry about that, I'm . . .

Leslie No, no. I think there was obviously a case of . . .

Roland Our fault entirely.

Leslie No.

Elizabeth Yes.

Leslie No, no.

Roland Yes, yes.

Leslie No, no, no. My fault.

Roland Splendid. Would you care for a little brandy or something?

Leslie No, thank you. It's a little early for me.

Roland Oh, I think we could all do with a spot of brandy, couldn't we, after . . .

Elizabeth No, thank you, Roland.

Mark No, thanks.

Roland Oh, all right. Suit yourself.

Elizabeth Do sit down, Mark, won't you?

Mark Oh, thank you.

They all sit

Elizabeth Shall we all have a cup of tea?

Roland (*forcefully*) No, no. We don't want tea. Nobody here wants tea, do they?

Leslie No.

Mark No.

Elizabeth Oh. (*Examining the table*) Well, what have we got here? Anyone care for a vitamin pill? (*She laughs*) No? Glucose sweet, then? Oh, these are splendid. You must have one of these, they're wonderful for energy.

Leslie (*accepting one*) Oh, don't mind if I do.

Mark (*also taking one*) Thanks.

Elizabeth Come on, Roly. Have one of these.

Roland Oh, all right.

They all suck their sweets

Elizabeth They're lovely, aren't they?

General assent

Roland (*after a pause*) Well, this is certainly proving to be something of a day, eh?

Elizabeth Yes.

Leslie Yes.

Roland And it's hardly under way.

Pause

Mark Going to be a mild one, I think.

They all look at him

Weatherwise.

Roland Oh, yes?

Mark You can usually tell early on if it's going to be dry.

Leslie Yes. You get to know the signs after a while. When you've lived in the country.

Elizabeth Yes, I can often tell if it's going to rain from the clouds.

Leslie That's one way. Yes.

Mark Pretty clear today. First thing.

Leslie Yes. Mist early on, too.

Roland Yes, so did we, I'm afraid. Both fast asleep.

Pause

Elizabeth I hope I didn't damage your crash-helmet at all?

Leslie No, no. Not at all. That's what it's built for ... Well, that type of incident.

Pause

Roland Anyone fancy a Bloody Mary, then? Now, that's a damn good drink at this time of the morning.

Elizabeth No.

Mark No.

Leslie No, thank you.

Roland Ah, well. (*Apropos of nothing*) It's a great life if you don't slacken. Weaken. Some people say weaken, I say slacken.

Elizabeth Weaken.

Pause

Leslie I really came round about the . . .

Roland The what?

Leslie The signature and the . . .

Roland Oh yes, the contract.

Leslie I'm assuming that it is a case of "Welcome back, Mrs Crabbe" and all systems go.

Elizabeth Er . . .

Roland Yes, yes. We hope so.

Leslie So there's nothing to prevent our finalizing things this morning, eh?

Roland Not so far as I'm concerned.

Leslie Good, good.

Roland It's just a matter of finding Mr Watson. Together with the necessary documents. He's still around, I take it?

Mark Yes.

Elizabeth He's shortly off.

Mark He's just getting dressed.

Roland We'll hang on for a minute, shall we?

Leslie Of course. (*Pause*) I think I was probably a little misled just now by the empty bottle.

Roland Empty bottle?

Leslie Of sleeping-pills.

Roland Oh, yes.

Elizabeth I must remember to get some more.

Leslie That and the note combined . . .

Roland Note?

Leslie (*indicating it on the table*) That one.

Roland Oh, that one. (*Pause*) What note's that?

Elizabeth That's your note, darling. You know, the one you . . .

Roland Oh, that note. I see. You mean, your note.

Elizabeth No, yours.

Roland Well, technically speaking it's mine now, but it was originally yours. I mean, when you wrote it.

Elizabeth No, you wrote that one to me.

Roland I didn't write one to you.

Elizabeth Yes, you did.

A pause. They are aware that this is not a conversation for Leslie's ears. He is none the less enthralled

Mark I think Elizabeth may be meaning, Roly—this life is not for me.

Roland Not for who?

Mark You.

Roland Me?

Elizabeth (*impatiently*) Yes.

Roland This life is not for me?

Elizabeth No.

Roland Why on earth not?

Elizabeth (*thoroughly exasperated*) Oh, for God's sake, Roland—excuse me, Mr Bainbridge. This note here. (*She thrusts it at him*) Did you or did you not write it?

Roland (*reading*) "I'm sorry. This isn't—nneeeur-neeeurr—neeeurr-neerurr—forgive me." No. Nothing to do with me. Not mine. (*He puts it on the table*)

Elizabeth It isn't?

Roland Not even my writing.

Elizabeth (*picking it up and looking at it*) Nor it is. (*To Mark*) Why did you say this was from him?

Mark Don't ask me, I've never even seen it. Mr Watson said it was from him.

Elizabeth Mr Watson? What does Mr Watson know?

Mark Nothing.

Elizabeth Exactly.

Roland (*to Elizabeth*) Not yours, is it?

Elizabeth Of course not.

Roland No, it didn't look like yours.

Mark Oh well, that's settled then.

Elizabeth No, it isn't. Whose is it?

Roland No idea.

Pause

Leslie Perhaps it's mine. (*He laughs but is stopped short by his sore neck*)

They ignore him

Elizabeth Do you mean to say I was woken up for nothing?

Mark Well.

Elizabeth Here we were, all feeling sorry for Roland . . .

Roland Were you?

Elizabeth I was practically blasted from my bed, Mr Bainbridge, by the most awful caterwauling coming through the floor.

Leslie Really. (*He laughs*)

Elizabeth (*laughing*) These three men singing like drunks.

Leslie Oh, yes?

Mark (*also laughing*) Well, we were trying to keep Roly awake, you see.

Roland (*laughing*) Oh, I see. You thought I'd taken those . . .?

Mark Yes.

Roland Oh, good lord.

They laugh

Mark You see, we went upstairs . . .

Roland Who's we?

Mark Me and Mr Watson.

Roland I see. Sorry, carry on.

Mark To see if Kitty was O.K.

Roland Kitty?

Mark Yes, she was supposed to be sleeping in the attic room last night.
Roland She was?
Mark Yes.
Roland Just as well she wasn't.
Mark Yes.
Roland Been a trifle crowded.
Mark (*laughing*) Yes. Anyway, I woke up Mr Watson ...
Roland Where was he sleeping? In the attic as well? (*He laughs*)
Mark No, he was ...
Elizabeth Elsewhere. He was elsewhere.
Mark Yes.
Roland Yes. Of course he was. I remember now, I gave him our bedroom.
Mark Right, yes. (*Pause*) Right.

A silence. Roland ponders

Elizabeth If you'll excuse me, I'm going to put on something warmer.
Leslie Yes, of course. (*He rises politely*)

Mark rises. Roland sits tight. Elizabeth puts the note on the table then goes upstairs. The men reseat themselves

> *Elizabeth goes off to the master bathroom*

(*After a silence*) Yes, we had the wife's relatives a couple of months ago.
Mark Oh, did you?
Leslie And we found we were doubling up all over the place. I was sleeping with her uncle for a couple of nights.
Mark Was that fun?
Leslie Well, no, hardly fun, no. I wonder where Mr Watson has got to?
Roland I wonder.
Leslie I don't want to rush you over this business, Mr Crabbe, in any way. It's just I do have to get to my solicitors with the cheque by eleven o'clock this morning at the latest. We've had one or two outgoings of late ...
Roland I know what we could all do with, you know. A Black Velvet. Ideal drink at this time of the morning. You ever had a Black Velvet, Mr Bainbridge?
Leslie No, I'm not so sure I should ...
Roland Come on and join us. Mark's having one, aren't you?
Mark Well, I ...
Roland Good man. I've got some champers in here, I think.

Roland goes into the study

Leslie Oh, well ...
Mark Can't argue with Roly. Not when he wants to give you a drink. No, the outstanding problem here is—who wrote this note. (*He picks it up off the table*) Once we find this out, we ... Ah.
Leslie All right?

Mark Oh. Yes.

Leslie Have you guessed?

Mark No. No. I haven't a clue. Just a touch of cramp. (*Flinging himself back in his chair*) Oh.

Leslie I should rub it.

Roland appears from the study

Roland I say, Mark, could you possibly rout out Mr Watson from wherever he is?

Mark Oh. Yes. O.K.

Roland It's just that Mr Bainbridge and I want to toast this deal and he's got the deal in his briefcase.

Mark Yes.

Mark goes upstairs to the attic, still holding the note

Roland Won't be a second, Mr Bainbridge. Sit tight.

Leslie Right. It's an alcoholic drink, is it?

Roland Good lord, no. They give it to nursing mothers.

Roland goes back into the study

Leslie Really?

Mark reaches the attic bedroom door

Mark (*calling*) Mr Watson.

Tristram and Kitty awake together

Tristram Er . . .

Kitty What?

Mark (*coming into the room*) Mr Watson, they're waiting for . . .

Tristram has managed to get half off the bed. He freezes

Tristram Hallo.

Mark I see. I see. Would you mind stepping out on to the landing a moment, please?

Tristram Yes. Sorry.

Mark Thank you.

Mark goes out on to the landing and paces up and down. Tristram gets up rather reluctantly

Tristram I'll straighten it up for him—er, yes. I'll—don't worry.

Tristram starts to put on his bathrobe quite slowly. Kitty, decisively, gets up, puts on her shoes and goes past him to the door

Kitty It's all right.

Tristram I think he—I think . . .

Kitty steps out on to the landing

Mark (*hearing her and turning*) Now then, I . . .

Kitty Yes?

Tristram puts on his shirt

Mark I didn't want you on the landing, I wanted Mr Watson on the landing.

Kitty Well, you've got me.

Mark All right. (*Grimly*) Now, Kitty, listen to me. I want you to be honest. I want you to be straight, do you understand? I don't want you to give me any feeble excuses or try to lie to me. Do you hear? You tell me the truth, Kitty. What were you both doing in there?

Kitty We were going at it hell for leather actually. Incredulously hard. Both of us. Bang, bang, bang.

Mark You were?

Kitty Oh yes. Excuse me, I'm absolutely knackered.

Mark I—I don't believe this. I mean, for one thing he's not that sort— he's . . . Oh, hang on a minute, yes he is. Kitty, what the hell's got into you? First Haverstock Hill, now this.

Kitty He's asked me to come and live with him.

Mark What?

Kitty I might. I might well. I'm tempted. He's very wealthy privately. He's got this farm in Camberwell or Camberley and he chases horses, did you know that? And breeds Burmese kittens.

Mark No, he doesn't. He works for Tacket and Winthrop.

Kitty He works for them? He nearly owns it.

Mark He's said nothing to me.

Kitty Why should he? He doesn't want you. He wants me. Don't worry, I'm realistic. I realize I'll be flung when he's filled himself in passing, but who cares? You got my note, I see.

Mark Yes, I . . .

Kitty Oh well, that says it all then. Cheerio. (*She goes back into the bedroom*)

When Kitty comes in, Tristram gathers up his remaining clothes and his briefcase

You don't have to leave, Tristram.

Tristram (*sidling out*) Yes, yes, that's O.K. See you . . .

Kitty Yes. (*Low, urgent*) Please. Back me up. (*Louder*) See you later.

Tristram Yes. (*He joins Mark on the upper landing*) Hallo. It's all been a—yes.

Mark I'm going to make an appeal to your better nature, Watson. If you have one.

Tristram Yes.

Mark Hands off her.

Tristram What?

Mark Hands off Kitty. Please. For her sake, my sake. I know that girl, Watson. I've known her ten years. How long have you known her? A few weeks, is it?

Tristram About twenty minutes.

Mark Is that all?

Tristram Yes. Sorry.

Mark God, you work fast, don't you? The girl's infatuated with you.

Tristram Is she?

Mark She refused to kiss me for years. It's—unbelievable. Look, she's a
nice girl. She's not very bright. In point of fact, she's extremely stupid
but she's decent. And I'd hate to see her flung, the minute you've filled
yourself. Like you hive off one of your unwanted kittens. So I'm begging
you. You seem to be a man who can very much take his pick so please,
go back to chasing your horses and do the decent thing.

Tristram (*eyeing him warily*) Yes, I will. Right. Certainly.

Mark Thank you. (*He shakes him by the hand*) Listen, they're waiting for
you downstairs. Mr Crabbe and Mr Bainbridge.

Tristram (*leaping into sudden action*) Oh lord. Right. Yes. Are they? (*He
begins the descent of both flights of stairs. As he goes, he manages to pull
on his trousers over his pyjamas, slip his bare feet into his shoes and
pull on his jacket. By the times he reaches the lounge doorway he is fully
dressed, if a little awry, and holding his briefcase*)

*Mark follows him as far as the first landing, watching his descent in-
credulously. He then goes along to his own room to get dressed. During
Tristram's descent, Elizabeth comes out of the master bathroom, now
fully dressed*

*Hearing Tristram, she comes to the bedroom door in time to see him pass.
She draws him into her bedroom, swiftly, unseen by Mark*

Elizabeth (*fiercely*) Not one word.

Tristram No.

*Elizabeth pushes him out again. She goes and sits at her dressing-table, does
her hair and makes up a little. Kitty continues to dress*

Roland comes out of the study with two full glasses

Tristram arrives in the doorway of the lounge

Roland Ah, Mr Watson. Just in time for a Black Velvet, come in.

Tristram Sorry, I was—sorry.

Leslie Morning, Mr Watson.

Tristram Mr Bainbridge.

Leslie Did we sleep well?

Tristram We?

Roland Mr Bainbridge, could I ask you kindly just to finish pouring the
other three of these? I left them on the sideboard in there.

Leslie Oh . . .

Roland Would you mind most awfully? I just want a private word with
my solicitor, here.

Leslie Yes, of course. Anything to . . .

Leslie goes into the study

Roland (*calling after him*) Just top them up.

Tristram (*opening the briefcase*) Yes, I've got all the—you see, I have the revised riders on the revisioned contract. I mean, the rider revisions.

Roland Yes, fine, splendid. On another matter . . .

Tristram Yes?

Roland I'll be perfectly blunt with you. I believe in that. I know that something happened last night between you and another person who shall be nameless. Now I don't want any details. As her husband, I'd prefer to be spared those. But just hear this. The fact is, as I think I told you yesterday, I'm a very successful man.

Tristram Oh, yes.

Leslie enters with two glasses

Leslie Here we are.

Roland (*sharply*) Just a moment, please, Mr Bainbridge.

Leslie I beg your pardon. I beg your pardon.

Leslie goes back into the study

Roland And make no mistake, I have influence. Not in all quarters maybe, but many. Let's just say, I could make life very difficult for you if you ever wanted to get into hardware.

Tristram Yes. Yes.

Roland Have I said enough? I can ride the storm but I doubt if you can. All right, let's get this little twerp in and get these things signed or we'll never be rid of him. (*Calling into the study*) Thank you, Mr Bainbridge, much obliged.

Leslie returns with the two glasses

Leslie Not at all. So long as Mr Watson's here to see fair play, I'm not worried. (*He laughs*)

Roland I think we might as well do all our paperwork in there, you know. We can use the desk. I'll clear a bit of space. It's absolute chaos. Somebody keeps moving things.

Roland goes into the study

Tristram gathers up the papers he has removed from the briefcase and prepares to take them through. He leaves the briefcase on the table

Leslie (*urgently*) Mr Watson, I know I can rely on you. I'm sure I can. Those little difficulties I mentioned last night . . .

Tristram What? Sorry, the what?

Leslie The difficulties Bainbridge and Sons are undergoing at present. The little financial hardships. I'd be grateful if you didn't refer to them in front of Mr Crabbe. Obviously in the light of his proposed alterations to this house, I'm anxious to gain his confidence—

Tristram Yes.

Leslie —and not to prejudice the . . .

Tristram (*moving towards the study*) Yes, yes.

Leslie All completely above board, I hasten to add.
Tristram (*going*) Oh yes . . .

Tristram exits to the study

Leslie Please don't misunderstand me . . .

Leslie exits to the study. During the above, Mark, now fully dressed, comes out on to the first-floor landing

Elizabeth comes out of the master bedroom

Elizabeth (*to Mark*) What are you doing?
Mark I say, Lizzie . . .
Elizabeth (*going downstairs*) Just a minute.

Elizabeth picks up her remaining suitcase and her coat from the hall

Roland comes out of the study into the lounge as she is doing so

Mark sits in the master bedroom waiting for Elizabeth

Roland (*talking back into the study*) . . . left it in here last night. I think so. (*Finding his cheque book*) Yes, here we are.
Leslie (*calling off from the study*) Mustn't forget that.
Roland (*seeing Elizabeth*) Oh, hallo, Lizzie.
Elizabeth Fetching my case.
Roland We're having a Black Velvet to celebrate.
Elizabeth It's far too early.
Roland All right, suit yourself. If you don't want to celebrate, don't.
Elizabeth Celebrate what?
Roland I'm just about to buy the house.
Elizabeth Oh.
Roland Well, try and look a bit more enthusiastic. My God, I'm only doing it for you.

Roland goes back into the study

Elizabeth Thank you.

Elizabeth goes upstairs with her suitcase and coat. Leslie's laugh is heard from the study. Mark is still sitting in the master bedroom waiting for Elizabeth. Elizabeth takes the case across to the bed and puts it with the other

Mark (*without moving*) Want a hand?
Elizabeth No. What do you want?
Mark I've got to talk to someone, Lizzie.
Elizabeth Well, not me.
Mark It's Kitty. She's made a set for this Watson man now.
Elizabeth Oh, yes?
Mark I've just found them in bed together.
Elizabeth Really?
Mark Yes.

Elizabeth Busy little man, isn't he?

Mark Well, what do I do?

Elizabeth Get in and join them or find someone else.

Mark I can't do that. Find someone else.

Elizabeth Why not?

Mark Because I—I've got all my plans based round her. I can't change them now. Too late.

Elizabeth Well, don't ask me to help. I have my own problems. Do you know, he's down there buying this house at this moment?

Mark Is he?

Elizabeth I can already feel it. Like a prison. Closing in.

Mark It's not that bad.

Elizabeth I'll be like the first Mrs Rochester. I'll go mad behind the panelling. You haven't got to live in it. You're free.

Mark (*snapping at her*) I wish you'd stop saying that. I'm not free. Nobody's free. (*He goes out on to the landing*)

Elizabeth They're freer than I am. They must be.

Mark I'm going to try and bludgeon some sense into Kitty first.

Elizabeth Oh. (*Wearily she sits on the bed and opens her case as if to unpack it. She stops and thinks*)

From the study, Leslie's laughter is heard. Mark reaches the attic. He knocks on the door of the attic bedroom

Mark Kitty? Kitty?

Kitty What?

Mark May I come in?

Kitty Yes, if you want to.

Mark (*coming in*) Hallo.

Kitty Hallo.

Mark (*after a slight pause*) Look, I thought we ought to, you know, just talk it all out. Once and for all.

Kitty Yes?

Mark Yes.

Kitty I thought we had done.

Mark Hardly. I mean, look, is the whole prospect just too awful?

Kitty What?

Mark Well. Me. And the fishing shop. And the—all the other things. It would be just us. Us running things as we wanted to run them. We'd be our own bosses. Wouldn't that appeal to you? All that freedom?

Kitty Mmm.

Mark It's worth thinking about.

Kitty Yes.

Mark Think about it. (*He sits on the bed*)

A pause between them

During this, Elizabeth gives an angry cry of irritation and gets up from the bed. She starts to do a few balletic leaps

Roland comes out of the study with Tristram

Roland I'll give Mr Miller a ring—and tell Winthrop I'll be up to see him on . . . (*He looks up at the ceiling*) My God.
Tristram What—what's the . . . ?
Roland It's my good lady doing her *entrechats*. Take no notice. If she drops through the ceiling, give her a round of applause. Well, cheerio, Mr Watson. Remember what we agreed?
Tristram Yes—yes—I'll . . .

Leslie comes out of the study

Leslie Good-bye, Mr Watson. Thank you for your services.
Tristram Not at all. It was, er . . .

Elizabeth leaps heavily. A cloud of plaster descends

Leslie (*looking up*) Hallo, what's that?
Tristram (*carrying on*) It was—it was er . . .
Roland I was just explaining. It's the wife limbering, I think. Or lumbering.
Tristram Some say limbering, I say lumbering, eh? (*He laughs*)
Roland (*blankly*) I beg your pardon?
Tristram Nothing.
Roland (*to Leslie*) Now, you see, there is a slight bow in this ceiling there. You notice it as she's jumping. But it's only slight. Now, I'll try and get her to do that in the attic and you'll see the difference.
Leslie Yes, yes. She could be useful. Floor testing . . .
Roland Oh, she has her uses.

Roland and Leslie go back into the study

Tristram, forgotten by them, sits and repacks his briefcase. A final crash above his head. Elizabeth stops. With sudden determination, she sits down, takes out her notepad and starts to write a note

Kitty I think—I think it's very flattering and wonderful to be the centre of someone else's dreams . . .
Mark There, then.
Kitty Even though you never asked to be there.
Mark Yes, but they're not my dreams. These are our dreams. I mean, we've talked them out. They're the result of all the long, endless discussions we've had over, what, five years. Should we go for this property or that property? I don't know—is it a good idea to stay open all year . . . (*Yawning*) Or should we be seasonal? All these things were more than just—just dreams . . . (*He tails away*)

Elizabeth finishes her note

Or not . . .

Elizabeth seals the note up and writes on the envelope

As the case may be . . . (*He is asleep, still sitting up*)

Kitty, after a second, lies Mark gently back on the bed. Elizabeth rises and puts her note on the dressing table. As she places it, Tristram gets up from the sofa, goes into the hall and starts putting on his coat. Simultaneously, Kitty rises and, with a glance at Mark, moves to the attic bedroom door. From the study, the sound of Leslie's laughter once more. Roland enters the lounge to collect the cigars.

Roland (*to Leslie in the study*) Now, you try that, Les. That is a single malt whisky and it's much, much mellower than that other muck we've been drinking. Now, that is the real McKay . . .

Roland goes back into the study with the cigars. Mark dozes. Kitty, about to go, turns, goes back into the attic bedroom and picks up her coat and suitcase. She goes down both flights of stairs and into the hall. As she is doing this, Tristram goes back into the lounge for his briefcase. He picks it up and turns towards the hall again in time to see Kitty opening the front door. She stands hesitantly, like someone about to jump into an icy swimming pool. Tristram watches her. Kitty takes a breath.

Kitty (*a secret, exhilarated cry*) Wheeeee!

She goes. Tristram considers for a second, then goes off after her. It is possible he will catch her up.

Mark slumbers on upstairs. Elizabeth meanwhile gathers her suitcases, leaves the bedroom and comes downstairs. She, too, reaches the front door. She stands on its threshold much as Kitty did before her. She puts down her cases and looks out. She turns and looks back into the house. She dithers

Elizabeth (*in frustration*) Oh . . .

The Lights fade slowly to a Black-out, as—

the CURTAIN *falls*

FURNITURE AND PROPERTY LIST

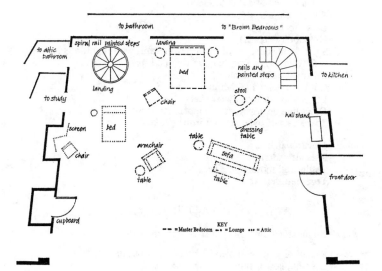

ACT I

On stage: LOUNGE:

Sofa. *On it:* cushions

Coffee-table. *On it:* magazines

Armchair

2 occasional tables. *On them:* table lamps. *On one:* box of cigars

MASTER BEDROOM:

Double bed with bedding and duvet. *On it:* open suitcase half packed with **Elizabeth**'s clothes, other clothing to be packed, handbag, make-up bag

Dressing-table. *On it:* lamp, writing-paper, envelopes, pen, bottle of 4 sleeping-pills, bottles of perfume, liniment, surgical spirit. *In drawer:* key, pair of tights

2 bedside tables. *On them:* lamps. *On one:* bedside book

Small armchair

Stool

ATTIC BEDROOM:

Small folding bed and bedding

Small chair

Bed table. *On it:* lamp

In cupboard: water tank, bucket, suitcase, small wooden crate, dressing

HALL:
Hatstand. *In it:* umbrella

Off stage: Spongebag (**Elizabeth**)
Briefcase with documents (**Tristram**)
Freshly laundered pyjamas, dress (**Elizabeth**)
8 large glasses of Scotch (including refills) (**Roland**)
Soda syphon (**Roland**)
2 sheets, pillowcase (**Elizabeth**)
Tin of peanuts (**Roland**)
Large martini (**Roland**)
Notebook (**Roland**)
Small blue suitcase containing trousseau, with nightdress full of confetti on top, spongebag, writing-pad, pen
Cheque book (**Roland**)
Cold wet flannel (**Tristram**)
Large glass of brandy (**Leslie**)
Dressing-gown, pyjamas, slippers (**Roland**)
Spare pair of pyjamas, bathrobe (**Roland**)

Personal: **Mark:** watch
Roland: watch
Leslie: full motor-cycle gear
Tristram: pen

ACT II

Check: *On dressing-table:* hairbrush, comb, make-up

Off stage: Packet of glucose tablets, 2 bottles of vitamin pills (**Tristram**)
Dressing-gown, slippers (**Elizabeth**)
Glass of tonic water (**Mark**)
2 glasses of "Black Velvet" (**Roland**)
2 glasses of "Black Velvet" (**Leslie**)

Personal: **Leslie:** large bunch of keys

LIGHTING PLOT

NOTE: The following plot gives cues where various lights are switched on or off in Act I. These may be supplemented by raising or dimming lighting in the different rooms as desired, in accordance with the facilities available: see p. 1.

Property fittings required: LOUNGE: pendant, 2 table lamps; MASTER BEDROOM: 2 bedside lamps, dressing-table lamp; ATTIC BEDROOM: bedside lamp, hanging lamp fitment (no bulb); HALL: hanging lamp; UPPER STAIRS: hanging lamp

Interior. A lounge, bedroom, attic, hall, stairs. The same scene throughout

ACT I   Evening

To open: Master bedroom lamps on. Hall lamp on.

Cue 1	**Roland** switches on lounge lights *Snap on pendant and both lamps*	(Page 13)
Cue 2	**Elizabeth** switches on attic lamp *Snap on attic bedroom lamp*	(Page 15)
Cue 3	**Elizabeth** switches off attic lamp *Snap off attic lamp*	(Page 15)
Cue 4	**Tristram** switches on attic lamp *Snap on attic lamp*	(Page 22)
Cue 5	**Roland** switches off attic lamp *Snap off attic lamp*	(Page 23)
Cue 6	**Mark** switches on attic lamp *Snap on attic lamp*	(Page 24)
Cue 7	**Tristram** switches off master bedroom lights *Snap off bedside and dressing-table lamps*	(Page 27)
Cue 8	**Kitty** switches off attic lamp *Snap off attic lamp*	(Page 36)
Cue 9	**Tristram** switches off lounge lights *Snap off pendant and both lamps*	(Page 40)
Cue 10	**Tristram** switches off hall light *Snap off hall pendant*	(Page 40)
Cue 11	**Mark** switches off landing light *Snap off hanging lamp*	(Page 40)
Cue 12	**Tristram** switches off bedside lamp *Snap off one bedside lamp in master bedroom*	(Page 40)
Cue 13	**Tristram** switches off second lamp *Snap off second bedside lamp in master bedroom*	(Page 40)
Cue 14	**Tristram** switches on one bedside lamp *Snap on one bedside lamp in master bedroom*	(Page 40)
Cue 15	**Tristram** switches off dressing-table lamp *Snap off dressing-table lamp in master bedroom*	(Page 40)

Cue 16	**Tristram** switches off bedside lamp *Snap off bedside lamp in master bedroom*	(Page 40)
Cue 17	**Tristram** switches on bedside lamp *Snap on bedside lamp in master bedroom*	(Page 41)
Cue 18	**Tristram** switches off bedside lamp *Snap off bedside lamp in master bedroom*	(Page 41)

ACT II Day

To open: General effect of very early morning light

Cue 19	After Curtain rises *Start gradual fade up to full daylight*	(Page 42)
Cue 20	**Elizabeth** (*dithering in the hall*): "Oh . . ." *Slow fade to Black-out*	(Page 72)

EFFECTS PLOT

ACT I

Cue 1   **Elizabeth:** "I shouldn't think so."   (Page 9)
Front doorbell rings

Cue 2   **Roland:** ". . . odd nut in the sideboard."   (Page 18)
Front doorbell rings

Cue 3   **Elizabeth** slams front door   (Page 22)
Door slam

Cue 4   As the three MEN kneel on floor to listen   (Page 26)
Cold water tank fills up very loudly: fade after **Roland** *exits to bathroom*

Cue 5   After **Kitty's** wailing dies away   (Page 27)
Clap of thunder

Cue 6   **Roland:** "I'll fetch it in a minute."   (Page 29)
Thunder. Raindrop falls in attic

Cue 7   **Tristram:** "Right. Thank you."   (Page 29)
Thunder

Cue 8   **Roland:** "Let's read her excuses, shall we?"   (Page 29)
Telephone rings in study

Cue 9   **Leslie:** "No, no."   (Page 34)
Thunder

Cue 10   **Mark:** "Roland? Roly? You O.K.?"   (Page 38)
Sound of running water from bathroom

Cue 11   **Mark:** "Sleep tight, old girl."   (Page 38)
Cold water tank fills loudly

Cue 12   **Roland:** "Frigid—irresponsible."   (Page 39)
Raindrop falls on **Roland's** *head*

Cue 13   **Roland** gets into bed   (Page 40)
Raindrops fall rhythmically on bucket and brandy glass

Cue 14   **Elizabeth** comes through front door   (Page 40)
Car engine outside

Cue 15   **Elizabeth** nestles in **Tristram's** lap   (Page 41)
Thunder

ACT II

MADE AND PRINTED IN GREAT BRITAIN BY
LATIMER TREND & COMPANY LTD PLYMOUTH

MADE IN ENGLAND